Why disasters occur & what can be done about them.

NATURE

&

DISASTERS

The connection between them.

By Celestine Ulasi

DEDICATION

Dedicated to all the people and communities who have suffered pains, loses and destructions from any natural disasters. The truth revealed in this book is inspired by the pains, losses and destructions you have endured for the future glory of all creations. May this knowledge build or strengthen your faith and re-enforce in you the hope of future glory of all creations.

Table of Contents

Chapter 1

NATURE & DISASTER

NATURE:

Nature is the force that controls and directs the essential conducts of human beings, animals or other creations and the physical world.

In human beings and animals, it is the inner force (such as instinct, appetite, desire) that acts as an influence on their personality or determinant of their personality. In the physical world, it is the physical force which is known to cause and regulate the phenomena of the physical world.

The inner or physical force that exerts influence and control over the world and its creations is the nature we are going to discuss in this book. The force within that makes them live and act in a pattern that cannot possibly change by reversal or retraining. For instance, human beings and animals go through training to learn and understand the demands of their nature and not to learn how to act in a way different from their nature.

The word 'Nature" has another use or definition. The word is also used to refer to all the earthly creations that was not made by human beings and to all the events and processes of the earth that are not caused by human beings. Things that exist or happens without human involvement.

These creations are nature but they are caused to exist or happen by a nature which is the one I first defined in the first 3 paragraphs above. These natures defined as creations in the above fourth paragraph have within them the nature which is the force that controls and directs them.

Nature is whatever that exists which was not made by human beings and there is another nature which is a force inside that direct and control the conduct of whatever that exists.

We have Natures and then we have a Nature within them that directs and controls their conduct.

For example, animals are part of nature which are creations because they are not made by humans. But as a creation, animals also have their nature because they have the inner force which controls and directs their conducts. So, though animals are nature, they too have nature (the force within them) that control and direct their conduct. This force within human beings, animals and the physical world is what I will be discussing in this book to reveal the truth about it and the connection between it and disaster.

DISASTER

A disaster is an event or an occurrence that disrupts the normal conditions of existence (such like the functioning of a community or a society) causing loss of human life, material, economic or environmental damages that exceeds the capacity of the affected community or society to cope using its own resources.

Disasters are seen in the academic world of the modern day as the consequence of inappropriate management or maintenance of risks. In other words, it is as the consequence of mismanagement or mistreatment of things that are potential risks. Disaster happens when things that has the ability to cause damages and loss are not properly managed or maintained.

Disaster is defined above with reference to communities or societies. This definition is rendered by looking at the small picture of disaster. Disaster is an earth affair and not just that of a community or a society. A community or a society is a tiny portion of the earth where the impact of a disaster can be at a given time. Most times, the process that causes disaster in one community starts from another community. For instance, a hurricane or torpedo can start its journey from another country or community but its disastrous impact will be in another country or community totally different from where it started.

The appropriate definition of disaster should be an event or an occurrence that disrupts the normal conditions of existence of the earth in general causing losses and damages that exceeds the capacity of the world creations to cope using their own resources. Disaster happens as a result of the processes of the earth and it causes disruption of the normal conditions of existence of the earth with evident result in communities. It happens because of the earth. We can be able to understand the

> The appropriate definition of disaster should be:
> An event or an occurrence that disrupts the normal conditions of existence of the earth in general causing losses and damages that exceeds the capacity of the world creations to cope using their own resources.

truth about disaster only when we see it for what it is by looking at its big picture and not communalize it.

This book will be discussing disaster with reference to earth in general in order to make clear why disaster happens and not just how it happens. It will reveal the truth about it and explain the connection between it and the nature that controls the world. This nature is the force operating the world of the earth and therefore has the responsibility to manage and maintain the earth.

EARTH

Earth is the third planet from the sun in our solar system in which humans and other living creatures live. Earth is referred to as a mother because everything in it was produced from it. God created the heavens and the earth in the beginning. Thereafter, every other thing that exists in earth was made out of the earth including human beings. Nothing that exist in earth came from heaven or another planet. Even the sky of the earth and everything in it were taken up from earth. These creations are what is defined as natures which exist and act in earth independently of human beings. They are called the earthly natures.

Earth consists of natures which are creations that exist and act independently of human beings. These natures that exist and operate in earth have within them a force that controls and directs their essential conducts. This force is their nature. The nature of these earthly natures actually have direct connection to the disasters they cause.

Earth through the processes of its natures has tremendous capability to cause disruption of the normal conditions of existence in it. This disruption is called natural disaster when they occur – a disaster that occurs naturally or that is caused by natural phenomena.

This reaction is called natural disaster not just because it is caused by the earth's natures but because it is a reaction of the earth's natures against the inappropriate management by the nature that controls and directs the entire world of the earth.

> Earth was created by God and it is good but the world in it was designed by Satan and it is an evil world.

Chapter 2

NATURAL DISASTERS

These are disasters caused by natures through reactions that are not controlled or directed by human beings (natural events).

Natural disasters are natural events which results from natural processes of the Earth and causes loss of life and severe damages to properties and the environment. It involves nature and disaster. It happens when the natures of the earth reacts to the operation of the force that controls and directs the conducts of earth creations whose responsibility it is to manage and maintain the earth.

Natural disaster includes all the geological, hydrological and meteorological disasters. Some examples of natural disasters are earthquakes, floods, storms, droughts, hurricanes/typhoons, tornadoes, tsunamis, landslides, erosions, volcanic eruptions, wildfires and other natural processes.

Many people see these natural disasters as an act of evil due to their ability to cause tremendous damages, destruction and death. Human beings are limited in measures when it comes to the issue of dealing with these natural disasters. Normally, human's best measures are to seek a better way to manage and maintain the earth so that its natures does not react with disastrous effect. The second is limited to evacuation plan aimed at avoiding or minimizing the devastation these events could bring when they happen. Both efforts and measures are never intended to stop these events because they won't.

Human beings have always been helpless in the face of these natural disasters because they lack the power to stop or avert them once they are on their way. Beside the biblical incidence where Jesus calmed sea storm by speaking to it, there has been no known human or spiritual intervention that helped to stop or avert these natural disasters once they are ripe.

What will be discussed in this book is not about communities or societies but about the earth or the world which is the single community of the entire human race. Earth is a single community for all human beings. Disaster occurs all over the world and affects every corner of the earth even where there are no human beings. Natural disasters are effects produced when the natures of earth reacts against the mistreatment of earth which is their mother. The society or community that lives in the area where it occurs is the one that will suffer most of the losses and the damages but the entire world will be affected by its consequences because the earth is one global human society.

In the above definition of disaster, it is stated that the affected community or society is unable to cope with the losses or damages using their own resources. They will need the help, assistance and cooperation of other communities. Natural

Natural disasters are effects produced when the natures of earth reacts against the mistreatment of earth which is their mother.

disaster occurs due to earth processes and not because of the society or the community that it directly affected.

Referring to natural disasters as community based incidents will not help us to understand why they occur and what can be done about them. Our understanding about natural disasters will be enhanced better if we know the truth about them as well as the connection between them and the nature that control the world in our earth.

LAMENTATION

"As evening came, Jesus said to his disciples, "Let's cross to the other side of the lake." 36 So they took Jesus in the boat and started out, leaving the crowds behind (although other boats followed). 37 But soon a fierce storm came up. High waves were breaking into the boat, and it began to fill with water.

38 Jesus was sleeping at the back of the boat with his head on a cushion. The disciples woke him up, shouting,

　　　

"Teacher, don't you care that we're going to drown?"

[39] When Jesus woke up, he rebuked the wind and said to the waves, "Silence! Be still!" Suddenly the wind stopped, and there was a great calm. [40] Then he asked them, "Why are you afraid? Do you still have no faith?"

[41] The disciples were absolutely terrified. "Who is this man?" they asked each other. "Even the wind and waves obey him!"

Mark 4:35-41 NLT.

The lamentation of the disciples of Jesus was this: *"Teacher, don't you care that we're going to drown?"* They lamented Jesus' composure which they perceived as nonchalance. They questioned if Jesus do not care they are about to die. They were gripped with fear and also worried that Jesus seemed not to be concerned the storm was going to get hem drowned.

Human beings are still lamenting the same thing up till today asking if God do not care about the fact that human race and the world is going to be destroyed by these natural occurrences. Many are wondering how some people could still believe in the existence or the reality of a powerful and loving God who is believed to be aware and have control over everything but still does nothing to stop these natural disasters or prevent their devastations. Human helplessness in the face of these events creates as well as fuels the doubt about the existence or the reality of all powerful and loving God.

Does The Earth React?

We all know both religiously and scientifically that the earth reacts. Science defines natural disasters as events of the natural processes of the earth. It occurs naturally without being initiated, controlled or directed by human beings.

Earth was created by God for a purpose. From the beginning, the earth understood what its purpose are and naturally responds to it according to the way it was structured and programmed. God used the earth to create things.

> "Then God said, "Let the earth bring forth grass, the herb that yields seed, and the fruit tree that yields fruit according to its kind, whose seed is in itself, on the earth"; and it was so. And the earth brought forth grass, the herb that yields seed according to its kind, and the tree that yields fruit, whose seed is in itself according to its kind. And God saw that it was good." Genesis 1:11-12.

When evil came into the world, the earth also got corrupted by evil and began to commit evil. The wickedness of mankind was not the only reason God sent flood that destroyed the world in the days of Noah. God said He will also destroy the earth with the flood because the earth too was corrupted.

> **"The earth also was corrupt before God, and the earth was filled with violence. So God looked upon the earth, and indeed it was corrupt; for all flesh had corrupted their way on the earth."**
> Genesis 6:11-12.

The world we have on earth is an evil world which was not established according to God's will and is not being run in accordance with the righteousness of God. The presence of evil nature in earth is the reason everything is reacting negatively. The entire creation groans in pain due to the evil nature in the world. The earth and all its creations groans because they are not fulfilling their true purpose due to bad and poor management of earth under the rule of Satan where all things are dominated by evil nature.

There are few instances where the earth was called upon to react. For instance, God caused the earth for the sake of Adam and asked it to produce thorns and thistles (Genesis 3:17-19). Moses called the earth to be a witness against the people of Israel (Deuteronomy 30:19). And God told Jeremiah to prophesy to earth to record as childless, Coniah (Jehoiachin) the son of Jehoiakim king of Judah. (Jeremiah 22:29-30). Earth naturally do react according to the displeasure of God who made it by responding to the presence and the activities of the evil nature. The earth does actually reacts the same way other earthly creations do because of evil nature.

Chapter 2

CAUSES OF NATURAL DISASTERS

There are two things that should be made clear here. The first is that God is not behind natural disasters but He has control over them. The second is that Satan does not arouse natural disasters and also do not have control over natural disasters.

These events are natural which means they are not instigated. They happens naturally as a result of the earth not being managed or maintained properly. They are the reactions of the earth's natures (natures of the earth reacting) to mistreatments or mismanagement by the world in it. They exposes the disagreement and incompatibility of the earth and the world in it.

As mentioned earlier on, disasters are seen in the academic world of the modern day as the consequence of inappropriate management or maintenance of risks. The risks here are the natures of the earth. These natures have enormous capability to unleash disaster if the earth is not appropriately managed or maintained to make them function in unison as naturally programmed.

Human beings are given the responsibility to manage and maintain the earth at the time of creation. They were given the human nature at the time they were made. Their human nature later became overshadowed by a stronger nature known as the evil nature. This evil nature then became the force within humans that controls and direct their conduct. By controlling and directing human beings who were given dominion over the earth, this evil nature also became the force within the world that controls its phenomena.

The overshadowing evil nature now is the force within human beings and the physical world that controls and directs their essential conducts. It directs and controls them on how to manage and maintain the earth. This evil nature is what controls the world in earth as well as human beings who has the responsibility to manage and maintain the earth.

Be it studying or training, the goal of every human activity is actually to learn and understand the demands of the evil nature that controls them and their world. Primarily, we go to school, study and train just to learn and understand how function with the systems of the evil nature. Human beings live and act in earth according to the control and direction of the evil nature. They do what the evil nature desires.

Omitting any reference to the force that controls and directs the conduct in humans and the world when defining or discussing natural disasters is done intentionally by researchers and scholars because they do not accept what cannot be seen. They acknowledged the truth that these natural disasters occurs as a consequence of inappropriate management of risks but they communalized these risks. These risks are the natures of the earth whose operations depends on how the earth is managed or maintained. These natures are the risks because they reacts disastrously if managed inappropriately.

The operations of these earth's natures are determined by how appropriately the earth is managed or maintained. The world in earth which is supposed to manage and maintain the earth is controlled and directed by a nature within it and within human beings to whom the dominion over the earth was given.

The earth was created to have a world in it by which it will be managed and maintained. The world that is supposed to be in earth is the world of God which is the world of the godly nature. It is a world that should operate under the kingdom of God. In this world of God, human beings are supposed to have the godly nature with which they should appropriately manage and maintain the earth in accordance with the standard set by God who made the earth.

The world that is in earth is not the world of God. It is the world of the evil nature and not the world of the godly nature. Nothing of this world glorifies God. Take for instance, the days and the months are given the names of idol gods. Their names are not related to God.

The earth was designed and created by God but the world in it is not under the control of God who made the earth. In other words, God's kingdom does not control the world which is presently upon this earth and as a result of that, the earth is being mistreated.

This world of the evil nature does not manage and maintain the earth because it does not operate by the standard of God's righteousness. It has proved unable to properly manage and maintain the earth. The world of the evil nature is actually mistreating the earth and this mistreatment is what makes the natural processes of the earth to become disrupted. When these natural processes are disrupted, they bring disasters. This disasters are known as natural disasters. The reaction of the natures of earth to the mistreatment of earth is what produces these natural disasters.

The disruption of the natural processes of the earth that produce different kinds of disasters happens simply because the natures of earth are reacting against the world in it. These disasters are the undisputable evidence that earth and its world are not in agreement or compatible. As a matter of fact, the natures of the earth are demonstrating or revealing the inability of the evil nature to properly control and direct the entire earth in unison as supposed.

The earth itself was created by God and it is not evil, but the world in it which was designed by Satan is what is evil because it is a world controlled by the evil nature. Satan is the Evil one. He invented the evil nature and is therefore the substantive ruler of this evil world. These disastrous natural events are the evidence of failed management and maintenance of the earth by Satan's world which operates in it and which rules over its creations.

Take for instance the incidence where lions and other wild animals reacts against their trainers or keepers. In some cases, they maul or eat their trainers or keepers. In explaining why lions attack their trainers, a British circus big cat trainer Thomas Chipperfield said:

"You can't afford to mistreat a lion or tiger because eventually they'll get fed up and show you that they're much bigger, stronger and faster than you are - and that can only end badly. But if you have respect for your animals and you're aware of their behaviour and mood on any given day, there's no reason why a trainer should ever get hurt." (***Thomas Chipperfield:*** Why lions attack their trainers. The Telegraph 2018 Sep. 17).

The mistreatment of earth by evil nature invented by Satan is what makes the natures of earth to react with destructive effects.

He opined that lions maul or eat their trainers because of being mistreated. These wild animals reacts against mistreatment by bringing such disaster upon those that mistreats them. Satan's evil nature mistreats the earth by operating systems that are completely disrespectful to the established principles that were designed to govern the earth. The result is that it causes the earth to react disastrously against everything in earth that has the evil nature.

Origin of the Evil Nature

God created the heavens and the earth to be managed and maintained in righteousness under the authority of His righteous kingdom where Christ His Son will be the head. Lucifer, one of the high ranked supernatural sons of God desired to possess the earth and rule over it rather than the Christ who God has chosen. In rebellion to God's choice, Lucifer invented the evil nature and used it to establish his own world in earth where the creations will be submitting to his evil-will.

Satan's major desire was to use his invented evil nature to properly manage and maintain the earth leaving God out completely. Evil nature was invented purposefully by Satan to oppose God's godly nature which God designed to be the earth's world that shall manage and maintain the earth. Example of this is today's human desire to create Artificial Intelligent (AI) objects that may become human substitutes in the management and maintenance of the earth. The depth of knowledge and understanding of the earth these AIs will have in order to appropriately manage the earth is left undiscussed.

The structure of the present world and the nature of its human beings was in response to Satan's plan. God's intention in creating this current earth in its present form is to make way for Satan to expose the evil thought he concealed in his heart while in heaven. For this to happen, God have to allow a time for Satan and human beings to operate their world with the evil nature so that Satan may prove his righteousness without God. Satan took the opportunity which evil the present form of creations offered to him to follow up with his plans.

Evil nature overshadowed human nature when Satan sold the idea to Eve that evil nature will give human beings the knowledge of good and evil whereby they shall become wise like God and be able to manage and maintain the earth without recourse to God. This was how Satan took over and established his own world of the evil nature in earth.

Now we have the evil world in earth and time is allowed for the evil world to prove its fit to be the right world for the earth. The earth shall be controlled by only one world at any given time. So, as Satan's world is upon the earth, the world of God's kingdom cannot exist in earth. For God's kingdom to come on earth as originally planned, Satan's evil world must be terminated because two parallel world cannot exist on earth.

To terminate Satan's world, there must be enough evidence to show that evil and evil nature is contrary to God's nature and to God's divine purpose. The evidence is simple – proves that their operations are ruinous to God's earth and its creations. Constant occurrence of natural disasters is clearly one great evidence against Satan's evil world. Due to the fact that these disasters disrupts the normal conditions of existence of earth's natures thereby causing ruins to God's creations and purpose, Satan's evil world has been proved as a failed system (world) unable to properly manage and maintain the earth. The evidence presented by natural disasters has proved that the world of the evil nature is an absolute failure. They supports God's plan and promise to end Satan's evil world.

The summary of what has been going on is that Satan created his own world or systems in God's earth with the claim and intention to manage the earth and rule over its creations rightly without God. In other words, Satan wants to show he has the same characteristics of righteousness like God. To prove Satan wrong and judge him as a rebel, God decided to allow Satan time to expose his concealed intention, reveal his unrighteousness and rebellion against God and His choice of the Christ as the one to possess and rule over everything in true righteousness.

The earth through its natures is reacting by these natural disasters to reveal the inability of Satan's evil nature to manage and maintain the earth in true righteousness. These evils are happening in the world because Satan's evil nature has not revealed any righteousness on earth. Satan's systems lacks the power and the righteousness to properly manage and maintain the earth and the earth is reacting through its natural processes. This is the true and factual cause of natural disasters.

Serves As Evidence & Sign

Like the sun and the moon, these natural disasters do not discriminate. They affect both righteous and unrighteous people, both believers and unbelievers. They damage whatever that is on their way both things considered religiously to be sacred and things highly regarded by the world. They affect all creations both human beings, animals, plants, lands, etc. Everything in the world suffer the negative effect of these disasters. They are recorded as evidence that will be used to judge and condemn Satan the evil one and his evil world so that God will bring upon the earth the righteous kingdom of heaven.

Jesus said that natural disasters shall be happening more frequently when the end of Satan's evil world draws closer. The frequent occurrence of these events serves as a sign that Satan's failed system and failed world of evil nature is nearing its conclusion. The devastating effect of these events will provide evidence that shall prompt God to judge and end Satan's world which is responsible for them. In other words, the more frequent these disasters occur, the more visible the sign of the end becomes and the greater devastation they cause, the more evidence is provided against Satan and his world and the quicker this evil world is getting to an end.

Hope and assurance that evil world with its disasters will soon come to an end is really a good news. Nevertheless, one should not erroneously assume that frequent occurrence of these events alone can bring the actual end of Satan's evil world. Disasters both natural and instigated will increase both in rate and scope, but the end will not come of Satan's evil world yet. The preaching of the true Gospel to the whole world is what shall bring Satan's evil world to an end for God's righteous kingdom to come upon the earth.

"And Jesus answered and said to them: "Take heed that no one deceives you. For many will come in My name, saying, 'I am the Christ,' and will deceive many. And you will hear of wars and rumors of wars. See that you are not troubled; for all these things must come to pass, but the end is not yet. For nation will rise against nation, and kingdom against kingdom. And there will be famines, pestilences, and earthquakes in various places. All these are the beginning of sorrows. "Then they will deliver you up to tribulation and kill you, and you will be hated by all nations for My name's sake. And then many will be offended, will betray one another, and will hate one another. Then many false prophets will rise up and deceive many. And because lawlessness will abound, the

> love of many will grow cold. But he who endures to the end shall be saved. And this gospel of the kingdom will be preached in all the world as a witness to all the nations, and then the end will come." Matthew 24:4-14.

God wants every human being to understand what has been going on so that they may know what His plan and purpose are. This understanding is very important because it will help people to believe in God's righteousness and accept His unchangeable choice of Jesus Christ as the one to possess everything. Whoever that will know this truth and understand what is going is expected to reject Satan's false claims and denounce the control of his evil nature.

Chapter 3

EFFECT OF HUMAN ACTIVITIES

It has been widely argued, assumed and believed that human activities plays major role in the occurrence of natural disasters. Natural disaster is defined as a natural occurrence, something natural which is not made by human beings but despite the definition, many strongly connects human activities to the cause. How true is this? There are two things we shall clarify in this chapter. It is whether human activities are the cause of natural disasters or whether they are what reveals the actual cause of natural disasters. We can make this clarification by studying how and to what extent human activities contributes to these disasters.

Understanding what human activities are and the type of human activities that are referred to in regards to the issue of natural disasters is very important. We have seen already that the occurrence of these disasters is a reaction of earth and its natures to the mistreatment of earth by Satan's world of the evil nature. Human beings are not directly mentioned in this definition because the primary reference here is the force that control and direct human conducts. Connecting human beings to the cause of natural disasters will mean they mistreats the earth by their activities.

Human beings are part of the earth's natures or creations. Creations or natures of earth are not the cause of natural disasters. They produce disasters as they react to the mistreatment of earth by the world that controls and rules over the earth and its creations. Cause of natural disasters refers to what causes these creations or natures to react with disastrous effect. As human beings are part of the earth's creations or natures, human activities can best be defined as a natural disaster itself and not the cause. Human beings behave the way they do because of the inner force that controls and directs their conducts. They engage in their activities to satisfy the needs created for them by the nature within them.

Human activities are the things human beings do regularly or occasionally to satisfy their desires, instinct or appetite. Human desires, instinct and appetite are controlled and directed by the nature which is the force within them. So, human activities are the things human beings do to fulfill the needs created for them by the nature that controls and directs them. Human activities are directly connected to human needs and human needs are created by the nature that controls and directs them.

The issue of human activities are real but it has been wrongly presented by scientists and environmental experts. Human activities does not fuel natural disasters. Human activities are part of natural disasters. Human beings like other natures of earth reacts to the mistreatment of the earth by through their activities. Human activities are necessitated or prompted by the mistreatment of earth. For instance, human beings would not have engaged in farming if God did not curse the ground because of the evil nature that overshadowed humans.

Human activity is instigated by the spiritual status of the nature that rule over earth and its creations including human beings. Natural disasters will still occur even if human beings doesn't do anything but are just fitted with the human nature and the evil nature. There will be no difference anyways because human beings does not act independently of their nature. They act only in accordance with the nature they have. Give them godly nature, they will produce godly acts and with the human and evil nature, they will produce evil acts. Their activity is directly related to the nature within them which controls and directs them.

Human activities are necessities created by the nature within them. This nature is the same evil nature that rules and controls the world of this earth. This evil nature was used to overshadow human nature when human beings connected themselves to Satan. This overshadowing evil nature created for human beings needs that require provisions for them to live day by day on earth. This nature mistreats earth and its creations disrupting earth processes thereby making life on earth very unpredictable for all creations especially human beings.

The disruption requires that mankind should provide for themselves everything they need to live and survive. It is the nature that created lots of needs for human beings. These needs includes but not limited to energy, clothing, feeding, housing, transportation, communication, education/learning, health, security/defense, protection from dangers and other creatures, wealth creation, savings, organization, governance, competitions, domination/supremacy, etc.

These needs manifested immediately human beings received the evil nature. Need for clothing and security was the first knowledge Adam and Eve received from the evil nature. They knew they were naked and that gave rise to the need for clothing. This need was not there at the time when they were unaware of their nakedness. They also became afraid of their environment and that gave rise to the need for security and protection. Can you imagine or calculate how much of human activities are involved to meet these two needs which have become enlarged and expanded so greatly?

It takes unimaginable enormous human activities to provide clothing, security and defense for human beings. These needs have been extended to even animals and other creations. Clothes for instance are made from lots of different materials such as leather from animal skins, cotton and linen from plants and other man-made materials like polyester which are prepared in a lab. Animals are killed to get leather, plants are cultivated in a large industrial scale using chemicals that destroy environmental health and synthetics are produced in the lab using chemicals which kills the earth. Factories will be built, machineries will be designed using unearthed materials and used clothes will be trashed or burnt causing further environmental hazards. The processing of providing clothing for human beings alone is far more than what I stated above. This is for clothing only. Housing, food, mobility, communication, healthcare, educations, etc., are not included yet.

Evil nature created needs which became necessities of life in this current world. To meet and satisfy these needs requires tremendous activities like construction, farming, healthcare, manufacturing, research, drilling/mining, fishing, building of military organizations and defense weapons, crime indulgence, wars to defend territory and interest, etc. All human activities affects the earth negatively no matter the type, quantity or quality.

Meeting these needs are what human activities are all about. From the time evil nature was introduced, these and many other activities are what human beings engage upon to remain and survive on earth. Due to these needs, human priority is not to manage the earth but to survive in it. Every human study, training and activity is focused on providing for their needs and keeping themselves safe and alive on earth. Rather than manage the earth and its other creations, humans are competing with these other creations for safety and survival.

Human needs came into existence because evil nature instead of godly nature is what rules over the world in the earth. Kingdom of God where every creation would have been fulfilling their purpose without creating needs or having needs is not what operates in this present earth. The effects of the evil nature are apparent to anyone who sees the gross mistreatment of the earth by these activities required to meet and satisfy needs created by this nature.

Human needs came from evil nature which is not the right nature for human beings and the earth. The scripture says we are strangers in Satan's evil world because evil nature is not the right nature for mankind, earth and other creations. Adam and Eve knew about the need for them to fend for themselves only when they received the evil nature. At that same time they knew fear and being afraid requires protection, security and defense. The first thing they did for themselves when they received the evil nature was to seek for food and covering for their body.

Human needs will always be there as long this world remains. Human activities cannot successfully be curtailed as long as human needs are there. Any activity the world may think and consider to be non-detrimental to the environment at the moment is just because the negative effect of that activity has not yet been discovered or that the effect is presently considered minimal.

Despite all the human activities that has been going on, no particular human need ever have received permanent solution. Human needs indeed have continued to increase, enlarge and expand both in kind, taste and variety. Most of the things that have been outlawed, prohibited or banned were once celebrated as a positive major breakthrough in our search for solution to the numerous human needs. We change solutions and not the need.

We develop new systems, new services or new products to replace those outlawed or outdated but the needs they satisfy still remains and they become even multiplied in some cases. The things we introduce to replace these old ones shall also one day be discovered to be as detrimental to life and the environmental or deficient to its purpose like the ones they replaced. This is actually a kind of cycle because human needs are insatiable.

These human activities are natural because they are essential to the nature of human beings. Human beings are victims in the issue of natural disasters and their activity is part of the disaster not the cause. Natural disasters are the activities of the victims of earth mistreatment. Activities of human beings which is a reaction to human needs along with the reactions of other natures of earth constitute the disasters. The problem therefore is not human activities and it is not the earth and its natures as opined by scientists and environmentalists and believed by some people. What this mean is that there will be nothing like natural disaster if the earth is not under the control of Satan who's ruling over it with a nature that does not treat the earth appropriately in line with the righteous principles God who made the earth established as the standard of its operation.

The nature that rules the world of this earth is the real cause. The world we have on earth is the world of the evil nature and the nature is what controls everything in the world. Everything that is used to run Satan's evil world has negative effect to earth and to the inhabitants of earth. Evil nature is a corrupt nature, so there is no way its world can ever be perfect. Blaming human activities shows lack of understanding of the truth. It is like blaming a boiling water and kettle placed on a burning stove for destroying the floor. The problem is the burning stove that heats the kettle making the water in the kettle to react to the heat. As long as the stove is on, the temperature of the water will increase and will reach boiling point at which it will start to spill out to the floor.

Human activities can never cease as long as human beings are fitted with the evil nature which creates human needs. The only way to end or curtail human activities is for human beings not to have needs. Human activities will cease if we don't have human needs. These activities which scientists and environmentalists are talking about are human measures to cater for their needs. The only way for human beings not to have these needs is if the earth shall be managed and maintained righteously. The only world which can manage and maintain the earth righteously is the world of the godly nature known as the kingdom of God.

"Your kingdom come. Your will be done on earth as it is in heaven." Matthew 6:10.

The kingdom of God is a world of the godly nature. Kingdom of God is not to make this world a better place to live. It is to bring new heavens and new earth in which there will be a perfect world where perfect human beings with the Godly nature shall live. God did not promise us a better world. His eternal plan is a perfect world. The difference and incomparability between what is perfect and what is better is huge. What is better is not perfect, it is not even comparable to what is best.

"And I heard a loud voice from heaven saying, "Behold, the tabernacle of God is with men, and He will dwell with them, and they shall be His people. God Himself will be with them and be their God. And God will wipe away every tear from their eyes; there shall be no more death, nor sorrow, nor crying. There shall be no more pain, for the former things have passed away." Revelations 21:3-4.

It is an error to describe human activity as a major contributor to natural disasters rather than a disaster itself. The real cause is human needs and human needs is a direct result of the reign of the unrighteous evil nature invented and introduced by Satan. To stop human activities, you need to stop human needs and to stop human needs, you must have to stop the reign of the evil nature and to stop the reign of the evil nature, you definitely have to end the existence of the evil world.

The fact that human activities are not the actual cause of natural disasters does not negate the effort being made in all fronts to identify the cause and provide solution scientifically. It is still a very reasonable measure that should be encouraged not because it offers any reliable promise. The one reason it should be encouraged is because such effort forms a vital part of human activities. Scientific research for cause and solution will not be necessary if these needs are not there. Searching for the solution will eventually deepen our understanding of the real issue.

The world of Satan is a world of constant and unending activities which are all vanity upon vanity exercise and the vexation of spirit from which we cannot be able to detach ourselves unless this world is concluded. It is like a journey on a rough road where an unlicensed and unqualified driver who does not know the way and do not understand the road is in-charge. Both the vehicle and those in it shall be affected by the inexperience of the self-acclaimed driver.

We are being compelled by needs to continue to pursue our activities even though we already know there is no permanent solution and no end to it. For instance, rich people continues to pursue money, save and invest even when they are not very sure they will live tomorrow. Most people keep working many hours even though they know that all the money they shall make will go into taking care of bills. People keep buying clothes even though they already have more than enough. Etc.

Human society always become deserted once you don't have much activities going on in it. A particular trade or business is abandoned or deserted by people once it does not attract much activities. If you stop human activities, you deepens people's problem. When government tries to use laws and regulations to curtail human activities, they end up creating more difficulties for the people affected. Socialism and communism for instance are systems designed to curtail human activities, but human beings with their nature cannot successfully practice any of the two because both systems does not address the issue of human needs. Human needs will grow out of control if you curtail human activities without having drastic control over human needs. This is why these two systems produces catastrophic effect in any society where they are practiced.

Some people think and believe that with regulations, laws and activism they can change what God has ordained and make the world a better place to live. They need to come to the knowledge of what the truth is. What has been going on is something bigger and deeper than what they think or what they can get out of their studies. To understand the cause and the solution to these events clearly differs from knowing how they function or operates.

Pursuing human solution to all these natural issues are part of the activities given to us in this failed world of needs. We are required to be busy and engaged in order to fulfill our purpose and perform our roles. Permitting us to be busy and engaged does not mean we are given the responsibility to invent solution to natural causes. Natural causes can only be solved by replacement of the nature. This is something human beings cannot be able to do. Evil nature created the problems but cannot solve it. The solution is a world of a perfect nature to come upon the earth.

The scripture symbolized this with the biblical Babylon where God exiled the people of Israel during the reign of King Nebuchadnezzar. Babylon was a strange world to the people of Israel but when God exiled them there, He gave them the following instructions:

> "Thus says the Lord of hosts, the God of Israel, to all who were carried away captive, whom I have caused to be carried away from Jerusalem to Babylon: Build houses and dwell in them; plant gardens and eat their fruit. Take wives and beget sons and daughters; and take wives for your sons and give your daughters to husbands,

> so that they may bear sons and daughters—that you may be increased there, and not diminished. And seek the peace of the city where I have caused you to be carried away captive, and pray to the Lord for it; for in its peace you will have peace." Jeremiah 29:4-7.

God used the exile of the people of Israel to Babylon to symbolize the evil world in which we live today, where Adam and Eve were sent to when they were driven from the Garden of Eden. The 70 years He gave them represents the number of years human beings will live in this evil world. This age was reduced from 120 years to 70 years. He also told the Israelites to carry on all human activities such as marrying, building houses and engaging in business while on exile in Babylon. Consider that God instructed them to engage in activities even though they will leave the land after seventy years. It is very clear they shall leave Babylon to return home without most of the things they will acquire or earn by their human activities but that notwithstanding, they should be busy and be engaged in the land of exile.

Another instruction given to them is to seek and pray to the Lord for the peace of the city, for in its peace they will have peace. This particular is even more significant to what we are discussing here. God's instruction to them was not for them to seek to make it a place where they should feel at home and become comfortable. The peace of the land of exile will not change the fact they are in exile. The land of exile is not a home for them. Seventy years in a strange land is like eternity because of the desire to go home. So they need peace to be able to pursue those activities and persevere through 70 years in that strange land. The instruction to pray here is not the same thing as praying that the Lord should make their stay in the city permanent or make the city a better place for them to live.

No matter how successful any human activity may seem, it is still a life of struggle that will never be considered a blessing to human beings. All human activities in this evil world are abuse of human dignity because human beings were not designed for such activities in the first place. God did not originally design human beings to have needs. All of human activities were born out of necessity to provide solution to human needs. Human needs are a creation of Satan's evil world and nothing about it or its success is worth celebrating if we really understand what God's plan and purpose are for us and the world.

> "This is what the Lord says: "You will be in Babylon for seventy years. But then I will come and do for you all the good things I have promised, and I will bring you home again. " For I know the plans I have for you," says the Lord. "They are plans for good and not for disaster, to give you a future and a hope."
> Jeremiah 29:10-11 NLT.

God's good plan for them will not be fulfilled while they are in Babylon. He will first bring them back home to the real land He promised them and there He shall give them a future and a hope – not in Babylon. Satan's world is the Babylon, a strange world of disasters to human beings. It is not the real home for human beings. Human beings are in this world as strangers. The end of disaster will not be in this world but when we get

> Human activities does not fuel natural disasters. Human activities are part of natural disasters.

back home where we shall have future and hope without vanity upon vanity activities.

Their activities in Babylon will not give them the peace and restoration they desired but shall make it easier for them to spend 70 years in Babylon. Human activities including all the research and technological developments will not make this world to become a home to human beings. Human beings will be at home when they receive the godly nature which is the right nature God designed for them.

Chapter 4

AGE OF NATURAL DISASTERS

We have record of some natural disasters which are given in the bible. The first of all these natural disasters is the flood which the bible recorded to have happened in the early time of mankind on earth. By calculating the time and the age bible recorded the flood happened, it can be argued by some people that this may not be the first natural disaster.

Calculation of Time and Age:

There is obvious disparity between time and age of biblical records and that of the world. How human beings calculate or measure age widely differs from the way God calculate and measure age. There is God's time and there is the time of man and they differ from each other. The difference is the reason we arrive at different ages when we compare God's report with human report of the same incidence.

God created time and season but no one knows when He began to calculate time and season for the world. We know why God created time and seasons but we do not know He sets them for His purpose. The book of Genesis chapter one only talked about days. It said nothing about weeks, months and years and did not say exactly how many days is considered as a year by God.

The story of the Garden of Eden did not mention anything about seasons such as the season of rain, winter, summer, etc. Human beings began to calculate age only after they know what it is and figured out a way to do so.

Secondly, God's given time and age often differ from time and age given by man for the same incidence because God calculates and measure time and age based on His power and ability. Mankind also base their calculation and measurement on their ability. Let's take for example the difference between the age of human beings and the age of dogs. A dog born on the same year with a human being will not have the same age as the person. 12 years of a human being is equal to 64 or 69 years of a dog depending on the breed. When a child born on the same year as a dog turns 12 years, the age of the dog will not be 12 years like that of the child. Depending on the breed, the said dog will be either 64 years or 69 years old when that child turns 12.

This will give us an idea of how the way God calculate and measure time and age differ from that of human beings. God's way is higher. When God said He did something in a day, human beings will look at the same thing and say it can only be done in 1000 years. What took God a day to accomplish will take human beings more than a thousand years to accomplish if it is something even possible to them. Mankind began to calculate time and age from the time Adam and Eve left the Garden of Eden and that was actually the time mankind began to live and act on their own according to the bible records which focused on the lineage of Adam and Eve. So, it is not wise or enough to use the disparity in reported age or time to argue against God's record or events.

The Flood:

The first record of natural disaster known to Believers and to mankind in general is the biblical flood.

> "Then the Lord saw that the wickedness of man was great in the earth, and that every intent of the thoughts of his heart was only evil continually. And the Lord was sorry that He had made man on the earth, and He was grieved in His heart. So the Lord said, "I will destroy man whom I have created from the face of the earth, both man and beast, creeping thing and birds of the air, for I am sorry that I have made them." But Noah found grace in the eyes of the Lord........ And God said to Noah, "The end of all flesh has come before Me, for the earth is filled with violence through them; and behold, I will destroy them with the earth...... And behold, I Myself am bringing floodwaters on the earth, to destroy from under heaven all flesh in which is the breath of life; everything that is on the earth shall die." Genesis 6:5-8, 13, 17.

> "Now the flood was on the earth forty days. The waters increased and lifted up the ark, and it rose high above the earth... and all the high hills under the whole heaven were covered...., and the mountains were covered..... And all flesh died that moved on the earth: birds and cattle and beasts and every creeping thing that creeps on the earth, and every man." Genesis 7:17-24.

It was a devastating flood used in the days of Noah to destroy bible's observatory world where Adam's descendants were. Adam and Eve were the first human beings created by God through Christ. Bible stories are focused on them and their lineage as the subject matter because God used them and their lineage to deliver coded messages about His plans, ways and purpose.

Mini Earthquake:

Another event recorded in the bible that reveals a natural disaster is the unnatural death of the three families which rebelled against God's choice of Moses. These were the families of Korah, Dathan and Abiram. A mini earthquake swallowed the entire family and their properties alive.

> "And Moses said: "By this you shall know that the Lord has sent me to do

all these works, for I have not done them of my own will. If these men die naturally like all men, or if they are visited by the common fate of all men, then the Lord has not sent me. But if the Lord creates a new thing, and the earth opens its mouth and swallows them up with all that belongs to them, and they go down alive into the pit, then you will understand that these men have rejected the Lord."

Now it came to pass, as he finished speaking all these words, that the ground split apart under them, and the earth opened its mouth and swallowed them up, with their households and all the men with Korah, with all their goods. So they and all those with them went down alive into the pit; the earth closed over them, and they perished from among the assembly. Then all Israel who were around them fled at their cry, for they said, "Lest the earth swallow us up also!" Numbers 16:28-34.

These are natural events which brought disaster and loss of life. They were both reported as something that was carried out by God. You may ask if this does not show that God ordained natural disasters. The answer is no. God did not ordain natural disasters and will not bring disasters unless as a response to the evil nature in the world.

There is something Jesus said to the Jews that will help us clearly understand the reason God permits or brings disasters.

> **"They said to Him, "Why then did Moses command to give a certificate of divorce, and to put her away?" He said to them, "Moses, because of the hardness of your hearts, permitted you to divorce your wives, but from the beginning it was not so."** Matthew 19:7-8.

The keynote is the statement of Jesus; *"But from the beginning it was not so."* The current earth was created to be a temporary place for the first phase of human existence because Satan invented evil nature which he planned to use to frustrate God's main purpose for creation. God's plan in the beginning was to create a physical world where He will place human beings made with the godly nature as the physical extension of His divine family and through them manage and maintain the universe in righteousness under His kingdom.

God's plan from the beginning did not include this form of world. This form of world only became part of God's plan due to the discovery of evil which Satan concealed in his heart before creation began. Satan planned and concealed evil in his heart while in heaven to be used on earth against God's original plan and purpose.

Evil was not part of God's original plan in the beginning as Jesus' statement to the Jews confirmed. Evil was invented by Satan who is the evil one. This made God to use His wisdom to bring a temporary world where Satan could have the opportunity to manifest his evil nature so that heaven should get to know Satan's thought and what evil is. This became necessary because evil was unknown and God could not judge and condemn Satan for inventing evil if evil is unknown and if there are no evidence to prove that evil is actually against God's will and purpose. I explained these more deeply in the book *"Origin & The End of Evil."*

In the two biblical events above, natural disasters were used by God to judge evil which is also rebellion. God unleashed flood because the earth and all its inhabitants have been corrupted with evil. His main target was the fallen angels who changed into human beings and married the human daughters. God send flood to wipe these angels out of the face of the earth but preserved humans who are from Adam's lineage.

The mini earthquake that wiped off three Hebrew families and their properties was a response to their evil rebellion against God's will and purpose. There was also the incident of fire that consumed the other two hundred and fifty men that joined

Koram, Dathan and Abiram in their rebellion. Their death was also a natural disaster, an act of nature not caused by people.

> **"And a fire came out from the Lord and consumed the two hundred and fifty men who were offering incense."**
> Numbers 16:35.

The reason these natural disasters happened was because they sinned. The scripture says that these two hundred and fifty men sinned against their soul.

Biblical Events and Records

Biblical records and stories are centered on Adam's lineage and on their world because God used them from the beginning to deliver secret and coded messages to His heavenly beings regarding the evil of Satan and God's plan and ways to deal with it. At the present time God is using the same records and stories to give human beings the understanding of His eternal plan and purpose.

Bible did not discuss events that does not relate to Adam's lineage because Adam, his lineage and their world are statements from God through which He reveals His plans, ways and purpose. All the events and actions described in bible are used by God to show what He has done, what He's doing and what He will do about the Evil one and his evil nature in other to fulfill His eternal purpose for mankind and the earth.

There are many information and facts which are not addressed or discussed in the bible because they do not fall within the subject matter. Bible does not deny the existence of such facts by being silent about them and also God does not need them to prove the accuracy of His record or report. The main reason bible followed only Adam and Eve's lineage is because bible contents are divine statements selected by God to convey desired divine messages. For that reason, it has to concentrate strictly on the actual subject matter only so that it will deliver the exact intended message without complications. The actual subject matter of bible is the restoration of inheritance to Jesus Christ and the establishment of God's eternal purpose for the physical world. God used Adam and his lineage to represent the good seed sowed in the world in accordance with God's will and purpose.

Apostle John said:

> "And there are also many other things that Jesus did, which if they were written one by one, I suppose that even the world itself could not contain the books that would be written. Amen." John 21:25.

> "And truly Jesus did many other signs in the presence of His disciples, which are not written in this book; but these

are written that you may believe that Jesus is the Christ, the Son of God, and that believing you may have life in His name." John 20:30.

Just as the above two scriptures says, all the biblical events written are also to show what has been going on from the beginning, to deliver the knowledge of what God has planned and to explain the ways God has followed to bring His unchangeable eternal plan and purpose to fulfillment.

God use events recorded in the bible to reveal that this present world is not the real world He planned for His creations. He shows that this world was created in its form as part of His plan to get rid of the evil one and his evil. To give guarantee that when our sojourn in this strange world is concluded, He will bring the promised perfect world which is the real home to human beings.

"For thus says the Lord: After seventy years are completed at Babylon, I will visit you and perform My good word toward you, and cause you to return to this place. For I know the thoughts that I think toward you, says the Lord, thoughts of peace and not of evil, to give you a future and a hope." Jeremiah 29:10-11.

God's thought or plan for human beings is that after each has spent 70 years in this world, He shall bring them home to a perfect world of peace void of evil and give them a future of eternity where their hope is fulfilled.

Chapter 5

NEW ERA
THE YEAR OF CHRIST

God appointed time and seasons for the earth in order to use it to determine the events of earth and its natures. Sun, moon and stars marks time and seasons for earth.

In the beginning was the era of creation when everything was made. After that came the era when the evil concealed in Satan's heart was exposed and manifested through human beings so that heavenly beings will know what evil is and understand its effect against God's nature and purpose.

After these two came the third era when evil and the evil one will be judged and the world (human beings, earth and all creations) will be exonerated from the role they played in exposing and manifesting evil so that God could establish His righteousness before the heavenly beings.

This era began when God send Jesus into the world. The coming of Jesus into the world was the beginning of a new era – a totally new chapter in God's plan for His earthly creations. The scripture says:

> **"For God so loved the world that He gave His only begotten Son, that whoever believes in Him should not perish but have everlasting life. For God did not send His Son into the world to condemn the world, but that the world through Him might be saved."**
> John 3:16-17.

God sent His son Jesus into the world as a demonstration of His love for the world. The world here is not Satan's world but the entire of God's creations which He used to expose and explain Satan's evil. God did not send His son to judge the world (His earthly creations) for the role they played in exposing and gathering evidence against evil and the evil one. He sent His son Jesus as a confirmation of His love for all His earthly creations despite the roles they played in His current plan. He did this to exonerate, regenerate and restore all His earthly creations who served in His plan to expose and condemn Satan and his evil.

This new era is what is known as the 'Anno Domini,' meaning 'the year of Christ.' We are living in this new era right now and then end of Satan's world shall come after this third era. It is a period that God has re-established His love for His earth and earthly creations which the heavens feared has been ruined because of the role they played in God's plan against Satan and his evil.

In the past before this new era (the year of Christ) began, God used to direct specific disaster to a particular people or community to respond to their evil or sin. Before Christ came into the world as the captain of the world and human salvation, specific natural disasters were normally directed to a particular people or community as a repercussion for sin or as a demonstration against evil done by the people affected.

Flood and the mini earthquake discussed in the previous chapter both followed that trend. They were specifically directed against those particular people as a response for their sins. Disasters was used as a judgment against the evil nature which operates in the world and not against the people through whom evil nature manifested its evil.

God told Moses the reason anyone who committed evil or sin should suffer disaster is so that such evil shall be purged from among the people. Death and disaster for sin or evil was used by God to deliver message against evil and not against the people of His creations. His goal was to expose evil and express His disgust about it. He does this through people because evil was designed to manifest in people. Reaching out against evil will make you to touch human beings.

This was the trend in those era before God sent Jesus Christ into the world to redeem the world from the power of sin and evil. After sin and evil have been known and understood, Jesus Christ came into the world to take away the power of sin to cause death. He separated death from sin and through his own death, he established death as a means of regeneration for all creations and no longer a consequence for sin.

The coming of Jesus into the world changed the trend of directing specific disaster to a particular people or community as a direct response for their sin. In the era that began from the time Jesus came into the world, disaster no longer serve as a direct response to a particular people or community because they sinned or did evil. Disasters is a general evidence that

> Reaching out against evil will make God to touch on humans.

exposes the failure of Satan's world or system that controls and directs the conduct of earth and its creations (natures).

Likewise, people no longer die or be subjected to evil attacks because they sinned. Sin has lost the power to cause physical death as a punishment or deterrence. The original purpose of physical death was for regeneration and that is the role it has returned back to. People die so that they will be regenerated through resurrection to receive spiritual new birth.

The death and resurrection of Jesus Christ brought judgment against Satan's evil nature and evil world. Death and resurrection of Jesus Christ made Satan to lose his position in heaven and his authority on earth. God told Jesus to sit at His right hand until He make his enemy his footstool and bring the entire universe under the authority of His Christ in line with His original purpose. We are now at the winding down of Satan's world and Satan knows he has but a short time. The final prove that his world and its system is a failure and unstainable for God's purpose is the reason we are indiscriminately experiencing natural disasters in the whole world today.

> "And war broke out in heaven: Michael and his angels fought with the dragon; and the dragon and his angels fought, but they did not prevail, nor was a place found for them in heaven any longer. So the great dragon was cast out, that serpent of old, called the Devil and Satan, who deceives the whole world; he was cast to the earth, and his angels were cast out with him..... Therefore rejoice, O heavens, and you who dwell in them! Woe to the inhabitants of the earth and the sea! For the devil has come down to you, having great wrath, because he knows

that he has a short time." Revelations 12:7-9, 12.

Presently, in this year of the Lord, Anno Domini, people do not suffer natural disasters because they sinned or because God hates them. The presence and the dominion of evil nature in the earth is the reason natural disasters occurs.

Evil nature has corrupted the earth and its creations. It has made the earth and its creations or natures unable to keep and maintain regular and peaceful processes. The reason these occurrence has become more frequent and rampant with the certainty to increase both in frequency and magnitude is because we are fast approaching the end of Satan's evil world.

For instance, when Jesus was told about some Galileans whose blood Pontus Pilate mixed with their idol sacrifice, Jesus answered and said:

> **"Do you suppose that these Galileans were worse sinners than all other Galileans, because they suffered such things? I tell you, no; but unless you repent you will all likewise perish."** Luke 13:2-3.

People or communities who suffer natural disasters are not worse sinners. It does not happen to them because they have sinned. How, when and where people die does not determine or prove their relationship with God. God loves all His creations and does not want anyone to perish. The only thing God wants to perish is the evil nature and the evil one.

These days (in this era), people do not suffer calamities such as natural disasters because they are sinners or because they are living in sin. This does not change the truth that whoever that is living in sin shall not escape the worst calamity if they happen to die a sinner and an unbeliever. We should not be afraid of dying and we should not fret over the fact that natural disasters are bringing devastations that includes loss of life. We should rather be more concerned and worried about what will happen to us after we die in this present life.

The greatest and most fearful thing is the second death which will mean to be cast out of the kingdom of God into the real evil world known as the world of hellfire. There is no amount of evil experience, calamity or suffering in this life that can be compared in any way to the condition of life in the world of hellfire. The worst is that the world of hellfire will last forever unlike this evil world which will soon come to an end.

The joy that should be in the heart of every human being is that this evil world is not going to last forever. It is coming to an end and all these evil and calamities shall pass away. No matter how we die, where we die and when we die, as long as we persevere as believers, we shall receive the end of our faith which is the glory and dignity of real human life that awaits us in the coming real and perfect world where we shall live the real life.

> **"Command those who are rich in this present world not to be arrogant nor to put their hope in wealth, which is so uncertain, but to put their hope in God, who richly provides us with everything for our enjoyment. Command them to do good, to be rich in good deeds, and to be generous and willing to share. In this way they will lay up treasure for themselves as a firm foundation for the coming age, so that they may take hold of the life that is truly life."**
> 1 Timothy 6:17-19.

Calamities of this current world happens indiscriminately by time and chances. They do not happen just because of anyone's sin and also not because God hates whoever or whichever city or nation that suffers calamity. We are all loved by God. All of God's actions and assumed inactions are a demonstration of His love for us. The only thing is that God works in a way highly different from our ways and deeply difficult for us to comprehend right away unless we are given the wisdom and understanding.

> **"I have seen something else under the sun: The race is not to the swift or the battle to the strong,**

nor does food come to the wise
or wealth to the brilliant
or favor to the learned;
but time and chance happen to them
all. Moreover, no one knows when their
hour will come: As fish are caught in a
cruel net,
or birds are taken in a snare,
so people are trapped by evil times
that fall unexpectedly upon them."
Ecclesiastes 9:11-12.

This book is specifically written to provide the wisdom and understanding for you to know the plans, ways and purpose of God regarding what has happened, what is happening right now and the future of this world. This and other books are made very simple because the intention is to sincerely convey the fundamental truth that will give the knowledge, wisdom and understanding needed for everyone to build, uphold and demonstrate faith in the face of all the evil going on in the world.

Human research reports are intentionally left out in this book because they are mostly opinions which changes as more fact emerges. Truth must stand on its own to retain its unchangeable nature as the real foundation for all other studies. Once you know the truth, you will see other things as human activities or opinions with which human beings vex their spirit as they pass their time on earth.

These days (in this era), people do not suffer calamities such as natural disasters because they are sinners or because they are living in sin.

Chapter 6

OUR TIME
&
SATAN'S NEW STRATEGY

I will repeat again that in as much as these events may be occurring more frequently now, the end shall not come unless the Gospel of truth which reveals what has been going on is preached everywhere in the world for people to hear, believe and be saved. The Gospel is the news about all of God's plan starting from the time before the world was made through our era, to the end of this world and to the establishment of the eternal world of God in earth.

Now is the Time of Man. The time God allowed for Mankind to repent and believe the Gospel.

Satan knows very well that no matter the amount of evidence gathered against him and his evil nature, his world will not end unless the truth is heard and known by all. Satan does not want his evil and imperfect world to end despite the abundance of proves of its failure and unsustainability. He is fighting back hoping to buy more time for himself and his world.

The amount of evidence required to judge and condemn Satan and his evil world has been gathered already. These enormous evidence has already been used to judge Satan and his evil world when Jesus died and rose from the dead. The time which God allowed for Satan to experiment his evil is exhausted and God does not give time to Satan any longer.

Satan and his angels have been cast down from heaven having lost their position in heaven and their authority in earth. One would have assumed that Satan's evil world is supposed to have been terminated if its time is over. In other words, why does his evil world still exist if he has been judged and condemned? What is the purpose of the time allowed for this evil world to still go on?

The time God allowed now is not for the reign of Satan's evil nature. It is the time for everyone everywhere to come to the knowledge of the truth in Christ Jesus. It is the 'Time of Man' which is the time God allowed for mankind to repent and believe the Gospel.

> "But, beloved, do not forget this one thing, that with the Lord one day is as a thousand years, and a thousand years as one day. The Lord is not slack concerning His promise, as some count slackness, but is longsuffering toward us,

not willing that any should perish but that all should come to repentance."
2 Peter 3:8-9.

There are new dimensions to Satan's strategy to retain the evil nature in this world. Satan has two major strategies with which he is working to corrupt the Gospel so that people should not hear and know the truth. He understand God's regard for truth and knows that what is required to be preached to all creatures throughout the world is the true Gospel and not just any kind of Gospel. His evil world will be over once the true Gospel is preached to all the creatures of the world. To extend the life of his evil world, Satan is using the time of man to engage the services of false prophets and false teachers to spread false Gospel.

False prophets and false teachers are being used by Satan to prevent the true Gospel from reaching the ends of the earth. These false prophets and false teachers are promoting false gospel which does not reveal to mankind the truth about God's ways, plans and purpose in regards to earth and the earthly creations.

The true Gospel will help everyone to understand what God has been doing, what He has done and what He shall do in the future to establish His world in earth for the good of all His creations. This understanding is the fundamental thing people need in order to have faith and hope in God's plans and ways.

False gospel focuses on this life as the ultimate chance by falsifying the intent of the scripture with the goal to undermine the credibility of God's truth and promises.

> **"And if our hope in Christ is only for this life, we are more to be pitied than anyone in the world."**
> 1 Corinthians 15:19 NLT.

The second strategy of Satan is to use the world political and economic systems such as democracy and globalism to install governments, organizations and leaders who will stifle the reach or growth of the true Gospel and frustrate the work of true preachers.

These organizations and governments shall make and promote laws and regulations which will criminalize the contents, language and the preaching of the true Gospel. The political state and society will redefine hate-speech to include the major contents of the Gospel thereby putting true preachers at the risk of being labeled and prosecuted as haters than lovers of humanity.

The goal is to stall the rise of true preachers and frustrate the preaching of the true Gospel. This strategy will give rise to the flourishing of false gospel and false preachers who will be ready to tell the people what they will like to hear and not what they need to hear. Motivational speakers encouraging the discovery of self rather than the discovery of truth together with fortune-tellers and reformed sorcerers promoting the spirit of mammon will become popular and famous all over the world. These will be regarded by the people as preachers and prophets.

> "Preach the word! Be ready in season and out of season. Convince, rebuke, exhort, with all longsuffering and teaching. For the time will come when they will not endure sound doctrine, but according to their own desires, because they have itching ears, they will heap up for themselves teachers; and they will turn their ears away from the truth, and be turned aside to fables. But you be watchful in all things, endure afflictions, do the work of an evangelist, fulfill your ministry." 2 Timothy 4:2-5.

Now is Our Time

I mentioned before that now is the time of man. It is the time which God allowed for mankind to repent and believe the Gospel. The scripture called it God's acceptable time for mankind. This time is part of the day of salvation and the day of salvation is when God will salvage all His creations from the evil nature.

Time of Man is the period God allowed for mankind to be accepted back to Him and be given the authority described in His original plan. It is the time for everyone everywhere to come to the knowledge of the truth in Christ Jesus. This time began after Jesus rose from the dead and was glorified in heaven.

This is the time we are in right now. Though all authority has been taken away from Satan, he still retained his wisdom. With his wisdom, he understands the time better than mankind. Knowing his time is up, Satan now deceives human beings into using the time meant for their transformation to cause more disruptions satisfying the desire of the evil nature which has overshadowed their human nature.

When the disciples asked Jesus if he does not care that they were about to die, Jesus rebuked the wind and asked them where is their faith.

> **Then he asked them, "Why are you afraid? Do you still have no faith?"**
> Mark 4:40.

The wind appeared to confirm their faith but they saw the danger and did not get the message it came to deliver. The same thing is applicable to us today. Many of us have been hearing the Gospel for years and have seen lots of evidence of the trueness of the Gospel through what has been going on in the world. But we complain about or against these things rather than acknowledge them as things that proves the Gospel message true. These things are what confirms the reality of our hope and faith in the truth of God.

Why are we still afraid of all the evil that is happening in the world and why do we still not have faith that God is aware and He cares? Satan has lost his power and time. This is our time which God have allowed for us to repent and believe. He want us to receive the true message which reveals the wise ways and plans He followed to fulfill His purpose for us and the world. This wisdom was born and kept secret before the world began but is now revealed to us by God's Spirit at a time when it is acceptable for all human beings to know about it because this is the time we can understand the meaning, depth and purpose of this wisdom.

God has control over everything and allowing evil and natural disasters is a way of demonstrating His perfect control and righteousness. He will use His control to end this evil world, condemn the devil and terminate evil nature to bring and establish the perfect world which we all desire.

Without God's management of the situation, we would have been completely destroyed. Even as it has been, God through His wisdom applies control over these natural disasters so that they do not exert their full potential whenever they comes. In His wisdom, He shortens their duration and reach to minimize damage and loss to His creations but yet use them to provide needed sufficient evidence against the evil nature.

> **"And unless the Lord shortens that time of calamity, not a soul in all the earth will survive. But for the sake of his chosen ones he will limit those days."**
> Mark 13:20 TLB.

God's purpose will definitely stand as it does not depend on us but we have a role to play about the time. God is infinite, He has no beginning and no end. Time does not control Him but He established time to count the days for Satan's world and our days in Satan's world. We have a very important role to play to

Satan's strategy is no longer to stop
the Gospel but to weaken and
corrupt the Gospel.

make this happen quickly. We need to believe and also get the true Gospel out to reach all creatures in the four corners of the world so that the end will come and there will be no more evils like the natural disasters.

Chapter 7

HUMAN PURPOSE & ROLE

One thing to know is that we all have a role to play to bring these evil world to an end. We also have a purpose to fulfill in this present world because we in our present form are a part of God's plan in our current phase of life. Human beings have role to play and purpose to fulfill in this temporary evil world.

Our purpose in this world is different from our role. Our purpose is to expose Satan's evil in the world and experience its pains and sufferings to provide God with the evidence to judge and condemn both Satan and his evil. Human pains and sufferings from these disasters are the evidence against Satan's evil world. God views human pains and sufferings as evidence that Satan's evil world needs to be terminated because God's plan for us is not evil but peace and goodness. Whatever that will cause pains and sufferings to human beings will be recorded as an evidence of failure of Satan's evil world.

"For I consider that the sufferings of this present time are not worthy to be compared with the glory which shall be revealed in us." Romans 8:18.

We are encouraged to endure pains and sufferings because they works for our good. Our pains and sufferings are the evidence this world does not operate by the righteousness of God and do not satisfy God's purpose for human beings and the earthly creations. God told Moses it was the pain and sufferings of the people of Israel in Egypt that made Him to come get them out of Egypt. If the people of Israel had been comfortable and at home in Egypt, they would not have been able to obtain the Promised Land. Likewise, without human pains and sufferings in this world, the hope of mankind to obtain the Promised Kingdom will not be fulfilled.

For instance, Abraham asked God to use Ishmael to accomplish His purpose rather than waiting for the promised Isaac since that promise seems to be taking too long to be fulfilled. He based his demand on the fact that Ishmael was also his son.

We are doing the same thing today by asking God to make this world a better place for human beings to live because in our mind the pain and suffering in this world has become too much and the promise of a coming new world is taking longer than we expected. We now seems to prefer that God should intervene and make Satan's world a better place for mankind. We do not think about other creations which are also waiting for the coming promised new world? The promised world of God's kingdom is not for human beings only. All other creations are also waiting for the coming of this world.

Natural disasters will cease permanently only when the earth comes under the control and reign of the kingdom of God which is the world of God's nature. This is when God will bring the promised new heavens and new earth which will be controlled by godly nature rather than the evil nature. Many are seeking for solution to these events because they think and believe human activities are responsible for them.

It is not false to state that human activities contributes significantly to the occurrence of these natural phenomena but not in the way human academic reports are referring to. The only reason human activities contributes to them is because the evil nature lives in human beings and manifests its evil in the world through human beings.

The evil nature is actually responsible but it lives in human beings and other earthly creations and operates through them. Even if the entire human race is wiped off from the face of the earth, these natural disasters will still occur as long as the evil nature still controls the world. On the other way round, if you destroy the world and preserve human beings with the evil nature, these events will still occur.

There has been some suggestions and discussions going on in some academic and scientific circles for human beings to discover another planet in which they can establish themselves due to the risk of the structural health of the present earth. The truth is that even if you should transfer the entire human race to another planet in their present form, these events will still happen there as long as they still have the evil nature. The situation of the earth has everything to do with the nature that controls and directs the conduct of earth and its natures.

For instance, we know that at the early time of the world, God destroyed human beings and other terrestrial lives and creations due to high rate of evil and corruption in the world but He did not wipe out everything completely. Earth, a pair of each terrestrial creations and all the sea creatures were preserved. Despite the destruction by the flood, evil has continued to reign in the world till today due to the fact that earth and those creations that were preserved still had the evil nature in them. Evil would have ceased if they were stripped of their evil nature that controls and directs their conduct.

God did not strip them of the evil nature because it wasn't His goal then to bring a new earth and a new world. His target with the flood was the angels who came down from heaven and transfigured themselves into human beings without undergoing biological birth process. He did that to get rid of these angels from the world because the earth was made for the sons of men who has to be born biologically. The destruction of that world did not end natural disasters because it did not remove evil nature from the world.

Rather than complain about the devastations of these events and keep questioning why God seems not to care that people are dying, properties and the environment are being destroyed, we should find out what role we are supposed to play to bring the right solution to these.

As already revealed, there is just one major thing which anyone who is unhappy with the devastations of these natural disasters should really do. That one major thing is the only role we have to play as concerned people who has the sincere desire to have Satan's evil world come to an end.

Besides having a purpose in this world, human beings also have a role to play to bring this evil world to an end.

Our role is to take the true Gospel of God in Christ Jesus and hurriedly spread it to every part and corner of the world so that Satan's world will be concluded.

> **"And this gospel of the kingdom will be preached in all the world as a witness to all the nations, and then the end will come."** Matthew 24:14.

As we have seen in the scripture that persecution and suffering was used to scatter the Israelites in the era before Christ so that they could bring the knowledge of God wherever they went. The same was done to the apostles and disciples of Jesus Christ who through persecution and suffering took the Gospel around the world.

"........ At that time a great persecution arose against the church which was at Jerusalem; and they were all scattered throughout the regions of Judea and Samaria, except the apostles...... Therefore those who were scattered went everywhere preaching the word."
Acts 8:1-4.

Creating human beings in their present form is a part of God's plan to expose and eradicate evil and its world.

Human pains and sufferings are the evidence this world does not operate by the righteousness of God and do not satisfy God's purpose for human beings and the earthly creations.

Chapter 8

THE PEOPLE'S EXPECTATION

God is presented to mankind to be all-powerful creator who love human beings and has the power to do anything even things impossible to any other creature. He has been described to have a purpose with the underlining goal of securing peace, safety, prosperity and comfort for human beings. This characterization of God is what make people to lament about evil and sufferings in the world such as poverty and natural disasters.

If God is both all-powerful and all-loving as characterized, what can we make of the fact that these natural disasters have continued to happen without any known sustainable human or spiritual measure to permanently stop it or at least make it occur without causing any damages? Should it be that God does not care that the earth and His loved human beings are being destroyed? Or could it be that the existence and the person of God is mischaracterized?

People's expectation that God should intervene in these situation to prove or affirm His nature of love and goodness is not totally wrong on its own. Many people are lamenting about the helplessness and vulnerability of earth and human beings to these events. Nothing is wrong with such lamentations only that it is based on ignorance of what is going on.

People's desire and expectation is that the all-powerful and all-loving God should step in and put an end to this disasters to prove He actually exists. This is the people's expectation but no one have considered it necessary to find out why God could not intervene in the way and manner we desire and expect Him to.

First of all, there is no exaggeration in the statement which says that God is all-powerful and all-loving. The reality of the earth and human beings confirms the reality of the existence of God. When people questions the existence of God, their argument really is if God is what and who He is described to be. It is never about whether God exist or not, but whether God is who and what others says He is. Anyone who wants to give reasons why he or she think or believe that God does not exist will definitely end up confirming that God exists.

If God does not exist, then there will be no need for proof. An attempt to prove that God does not exist is by itself a confirmation that there is God. Generally, you can only try to disprove something that could likely be a reality. God truly exist and He is all-powerful and all-loving. The issue is that human beings does not understand the ways and thoughts of God which is very different from ours.

Unlike human beings and the things human beings are conversant with, God deploys His power and His love for His own pleasure, to serve His glorious purpose only. He does not deploy His power just to show He has power, but He does it to prove that His purpose will always stand. The ability to make His will prevail and His purpose stand at all times is the actual quality that make God who and what He is.

God can play strong, mighty or weak in order for His will to prevail and for His purpose to stand. That is what being all-powerful or almighty means – it is being able to do all things whether big or small, strong or weak, etc., without failing in purpose. Being all-powerful does not mean being able to do only big and strong things. It means being able to do what it will take at all times to make sure your will prevails and your purpose stands. For instance, Jesus humbled himself to the point of death on a stake just for the will of God to prevail and for God's purpose to stand.

> **"Therefore My Father loves Me, because I lay down My life that I may take it again. No one takes it from Me, but I lay it down of Myself. I have power to lay it down, and I have power to take it again. This command I have received from My Father."** John 10:17-18.

These natural disasters serves God's purpose. They reveals God's righteousness and exposes Satan's unrighteousness. In the scripture, God called locust, caterpillar, palmer worm and canker worm His soldiers. These are destroyers whose destructive works serves to establish God's righteousness against Satan's evil nature. This may sound very absurd to many because there is nothing terrestrially good about natural disasters and destructions. Natural disasters are called disasters because they are devastating. How could any kind of devastation be related to all-loving and caring God? Remember that whatever works against your enemy works to your favour. Therefore, these natural disasters which works against Satan's world to expose its incapability and unrighteousness are really a great favour to God's plan and purpose.

As we already know, the presence of the world of evil nature in earth is the cause of natural disasters. Since God is not the ruler of this world, it does not pose any moral obligation to God to prove Himself powerful and loving by stopping these events. Evil nature was invented as a challenge to God's sovereignty and absolutism. Satan's goal is to prove that earth can be managed and maintained properly without adherence to God's standard. Failed management and maintenance of the earth by Satan's world is the cause of the disruption of the earth processes whose effect are the natural disasters.

People's desire for God to intervene in the way and manner that meet their expectation simply means asking God to do something that will greatly support Satan's claim against Him. Such intervention will be God helping Satan's cause. It is the same as asking God to testify against Himself and act against His own purpose.

That God has not made these disasters to cease does not mean He is not all-powerful or that He does not love human beings and the earth which are suffering the destructive effect of these disasters. What it shows is that doing so will not serve His good purpose since these natural disasters reveals God's righteousness by exposing the failure of Satan's unrighteous world controlled by the evil nature.

Many religious people have also joined the bandwagon of praying to God to make this world a better place to live. What these people seems to forget is that their prayer is a request to God to hand victory to Satan. For God to make this world a better place is for Him to put His righteousness upon Satan so that Satan's world will remain forever and the righteous kingdom of Christ the chosen one of God should not come. This is asking God to give the inheritance to Satan who schemed to usurp them rather than fulfill His promise that the Christ shall inherit everything.

Abraham acted in this same way even after he has demonstrated uncommon faith in God by believing God's promise that Isaac shall inherit the covenant. After waiting for many years for the promised Isaac to come, he asked that God should rather take Ishmael as the one to inherit the covenant since Ishmael also is his son.

God said to him that the covenant is for the son his wife Sarah shall bear for him. Abraham was happy he has already become a biological father. God's promise for Isaac was not just to make Abraham a biological father. The promise was for God's own purpose and fulfilling it remains a top priority to God. God said He will bless Ishmael, multiply him and make him fruitful because Ismael also is Abraham's son but He insisted that Isaac as a promise must be fulfilled. In this way God showed that His promise to give Abraham a son is for a purpose very different from Abraham's understanding and desire.

"Then Abraham fell on his face and laughed, and said in his heart, "Shall a child be born to a man who is one hundred years old? And shall Sarah, who is ninety years old, bear a child?" And Abraham said to God, "Oh, that Ishmael might live before You!" Then God said: "No, Sarah your wife shall bear you a son, and you shall call his name Isaac; I will establish My covenant with him for an everlasting covenant, and with his descendants after him. And as for Ishmael, I have heard you. Behold, I have blessed him, and will make him fruitful, and will multiply him exceedingly. He shall beget twelve princes, and I will make him a great nation. But My covenant I

> will establish with Isaac, whom Sarah
> shall bear to you at this set time next
> year." Then He finished -talking with
> him, and God went up from Abraham."
> Genesis 17:17-22.

Likewise, God's promise of new heavens and a new earth was not just to give us a better world. It is for a purpose far bigger, greater and higher than our desire for a better place. It is more about God's righteousness, sovereignty and absolutism.

God had a purpose for which He planned for physical creations to be made and for Christ to inherit them. He promised that Christ will possess everything that shall be created. He made this plan and gave this promise even before the world and human beings were made.

Satan invented evil nature to frustrate this plan and promise of God. So, asking God to make this world in its form a better place for human beings to live is a gross demonstration of human selfishness and ignorance of the Gospel truth. Human beings always think and believe everything is about themselves. No, it is always about God Himself who made everything for His own pleasure.

God did not ordain natural disasters even though He has power over it and can exercise control over them. Though they occur as a response and reaction of earth to Satan's evil nature that rules in the world, nevertheless, Satan do not have control over them and cannot use them to advance his cause. Natural disasters are working against Satan's plan and purpose. They are doing great damages to Satan's cause. Satan would love to stop them if he has the power because their occurrence is an evidence against him and against his world.

Our expectations of God in regards to evil things happening in the world is born out of sheer ignorance of the truth about what has been going on.

God truly exist and He is all-powerful and all-loving. The issue is that human beings does not understand the ways and thoughts of God which is very different from ours.

Chapter 9

THE REAL SOLUTION

Solution is a particular method to solve a problem or an answer to a problem. A problem will be considered solvable if there is a solution. The question here is whether natural disasters or evil in the world has a solution?

Solution to a problem is different from the cause of the problem. We know what causes natural disasters and also the one responsible for what causes natural disasters. If there is solution to natural disasters, then we need to find out what the solution is and who has the solution? This will help us to determine if there is anything anyone can do to stop natural disasters from happening.

There is a solution to natural disasters for sure. Just the way it is with other issues, when the cause is determined and identified, the hope and certainty for solution is there. Understanding the cause of an issue makes it possible to determine what the solution is or will be. You can't have a real solution if you don't know the actual cause.

It is clear human beings are not the cause of natural disasters. However, it has been established here that inevitable human activities together with that of all other creations are completely part of natural disasters and not the cause. That human existence and survival in this present phase is tightly connected to earth and other earthly natures is the fact which has made finding solution to natural disasters to be viewed as the responsibility of human beings.

Another factor towards this line of thought is the fact that human beings are the ones God gave dominion over the earth to maintain and manage it. For the above two reasons, the responsibility to find solution to natural disasters is somehow considered to fall on human beings rather than on any other creation.

Though dominion of the earth was given to human beings, it is a clear fact they never had dominion over the earth. They do not have dominion and they do not have control over the earth. The reason for this is because they do not have the right nature of God's righteousness to exercise dominion over the earth.

Human nature and the evil nature does not have God's righteousness which is required for any creation to have dominion and exercise control successfully over the earth. Dominion and control over the earth can only be done by creations with the godly nature. Human beings in their current form do not have the godly nature.

The earth was made in its present form to allow Satan to take over dominion and expose his evil nature which he concealed in his heart while in heaven. Satan seized the opportunity offered by the earth's form, took over dominion of the earth and has been the one managing it in a way totally different from the righteous way ordained by God who made the earth. Satan's dominion over the earth is the actual reason we are having natural disasters.

Human effort to solve natural disasters is not out of place at all. Seeking for solution of something will enable you to get better understanding of the problem and its cause. It will draw you to the deeper knowledge and understanding which cannot be received through wishful thinking only.

For instance, Moses' was drawn to God by his determination to find out how a tree could literally be on fire but does not actually get burnt. He got deeper knowledge and understanding of God's solution to the suffering of the people of Israel in Egypt when he drew near. His search for a cause brought him to God and from God he got the solution he has been looking for since his youth.

> "I know that whatever God does, it shall be forever. Nothing can be added to it, and nothing taken from it. God does it, that men should fear before Him. That which is has already been, and what is to be has already been;

And God requires an account of what is past." Ecclesiastes 3:14-15.

Every single problem in the world already has a solution that is why they could even happen. Nothing will happen in this world if there is no solution already for it. God already has solution for whatever He allows to happen in the world.

God's plan and purpose to establish a perfect world for perfect human beings is what shall be forever. Evil shall not be added to this plan and peace shall not be subtracted from it. Satan rebelliously invented evil to add it to what God has designed. God brought a temporary earth to defeat Satan's evil design so that it will not affect God's eternal plan. Men shall fear God and will desire His righteousness when they see and understand God already has solution for all the effects of Satan's evil nature in the world.

God does not make these things that happens again and again to happen. He only allows them to happen as a record of account to be used to judge this evil world and the ruler of this evil world. The ultimate solution to these things that keeps happening is with God. Human quest for solution to natural disasters is a very welcome effort in the right direction. The only thing is that they do not seem to fully understand what they are supposed to discover by searching for solution. They are not expected to solve them through their searching, rather, it is expected they will find God and understand His planned solution to these.

Human beings are expected to find God when they search for solution to natural disasters and to any of the world and human problems for that matter. This was exactly what happened to Moses. The solution to natural disaster is the same one solution to overall human and world problems.

All what God want everyone to understand is that the present kind of human beings and the current world in its present form are imperfect in nature and therefore cannot possibly be problem-free. God want everyone to know this so that with reverence fear people may seek Him to bring His own perfect world which is the only solution to all the world and human problems.

You can't solve natural disasters as something separate from human nature and the nature of the world. The nature of the present kind of human beings and the nature of the present world are both imperfect. Natural disasters are happening as a result of the imperfect nature of human beings and the imperfect nature of the world that is upon the earth. Imperfect human nature and imperfect world cannot manage and maintain the earth in the righteous way ordained by God who made and established the earth. Natural disasters will cease forever if you make perfect the nature of human beings and the nature of the world that is upon the earth.

Natural disasters occurs because the earth reacts to the unrighteousness of the world that operates in earth. The only thing that will make human beings and the world perfect is the righteousness of God. Righteousness of God is the only real solution to all natural disasters no matter the name and their description. God's righteousness is all the earth need to have and maintain a peaceful process that will never be disrupted to cause disaster.

The righteousness of God will be established on earth only when the kingdom of God comes upon the earth. Human beings are expected to discover the righteousness of God when they search for solution to natural disasters. The righteousness of God is revealed in Jesus Christ the one God has chosen and sent from heaven. He is the one who shall rule over the earth in righteousness. Whoever that desires to be part of the perfect world must submit himself or herself to receive God's righteousness by receiving Jesus Christ. The world (heavens and the earth) have received Jesus Christ and therefore is saved to be recreated as a perfect world. Anyone who receives Jesus Christ will be saved to be regenerated through new spiritual birth just like the heavens and the earth that shall be made new.

> **"You search the Scriptures, for in them you think you have eternal life; and these are they which testify of Me. But you are not willing to come to Me that you may have life."** John 5:39-40.

The Jews search the scriptures to find eternal life in it but not knowing the scripture will only point them to Jesus in who is the eternal life they're looking for. Searching the scripture does not provide the solution, it leads people to the one who has the solution. Jesus demonstrated his power over natural disasters when he rebuked the storm and commanded it to cease. He did not arrange for evacuation and did not advise for a change of route. He spoke to the sea and the storm stopped because he has the authority that could solve it.

> **"Now when they had left the multitude, they took Him along in the boat as He was. And other little boats were also with Him. And a great windstorm arose, and the waves beat into the boat, so that it was already filling. But He was in the stern, asleep on a pillow. And they awoke Him and said to Him, "Teacher, do You not care that we are perishing?" Then He arose and rebuked the wind, and said to the sea, "Peace, be still!" And the wind ceased and there was a great calm." Mark 4:36-39.**

This is different from what happened to the boat that was transporting Paul to Rome which was also caught in a storm. In the book of Acts 27, Luke gave details of that journey and the disaster they suffered from the sea storm. Paul first advised them about the storm saying;

> "Men, I perceive that this voyage will end with disaster and much loss, not only of the cargo and ship, but also our lives." Acts 27:10.

These men were professionals and experienced sailors with expert knowledge of the sea and storms. They took many measures to overcome the storm and when their experience and expertise proved unsuccessful they did what men normally do – abandon the ship and escape.

> "Then, fearing lest we should run aground on the rocks, they dropped four anchors from the stern, and prayed for day to come. And as the sailors were seeking to escape from the ship, when they had let down the skiff into the sea, under pretense of putting out anchors from the prow, Paul said to the centurion and the soldiers, "Unless these men stay in the ship, you cannot be saved." Acts 27:29-30.

Paul did not condemn all the efforts made by the sailors to overcome the storm. Human efforts and measures no matter how good they may be can only help to manage the effect of these events. They do not serve as real solution and should not be considered as measures to overcome them. They cannot make them not to happen again.

Everyone in that boat was gripped by fear except Paul. The reason Paul was not afraid or perturbed by the impending natural disaster was because he received information from God's angel and he knew that only God has the solution to natural disasters. They would have overcome had they believed Paul who was informed by the one who has solution to natural disasters (Acts 27:21-26). We conduct search or research to be informed. We either search for what is in existence but is unknown to us or to be informed on how to use what is in existence to create what is needed. The one who will inform us is the one who has the solution. We do not search to create solution because there is solution already for all problems. We search to be informed about solutions and about how to handle solutions.

Likewise, all academic researches (scientific and social) are not meant to provide real solution to natural disasters. They are supposed to help us to know and understand God, the one who has solutions and who alone can inform us on how to apply solutions. What we expect from our researches, studies, regulations and investments is for them to lead us to the one who has all solutions.

As a matter of fact, everything we invented and applied as a solution to natural disasters are themselves part of human activities we blame to be fueling these events. While we continue in our human efforts to minimize or avoid the impact of these disasters, the right thing is to understand that the expected goal of our search is to seek God who alone has the solution.

It is highly recommended that we keep searching for solution to natural disasters, but we must understand what we are expected to discover. We are expected to discover God who alone has the solution to these events. As we discover God through our search, we will understand what His solution is. This discovery will help us to have faith in Him and live with the assured hope to see the fulfillment of His unchanging plan which shall eradicate natural disasters in the coming real world.

People are worried about the future of the earth and are advocating for different ideas on what should be done to sustain the earth. This is somehow funny because human beings do not live forever in this world. They have lifespan and dies at the end of their lifespan. What then is the motivation for human beings to be seeking for a lasting solution in a world in which they too cannot last forever? Human beings do not exist for the world. It is the world that exist for human beings. So, if human beings cannot live forever in this world, then the world itself cannot last forever.

Those who search for solutions in this world are really the ones who are supposed to develop a sustainable faith in God because searching for solution to natural disasters brings humans face to face with truth about God and His plans. Truth sets the record straight regarding all the false accusations of the enemy against mankind and against God. Satan does not want the blame to be

> Human nature and the evil nature does not have God's righteousness which is required for any creation to have dominion and exercise control successfully over the earth.

upon him, so he falsely shifts the blame to mankind and to God.

Discovering the truth will make human beings free from all fears especially about their future and about all these natural events. They will clearly understand that these events spells doom only for Satan and his world and not for mankind.

When Will Natural Disasters Cease?

Natural disaster will not only stop, it will cease to exist when human beings and the world receive the perfect godly nature. That is when God's righteousness is established upon the earth. With the human nature, human beings are just the sons of men, but with the godly nature, they will become the sons of God.

Earth was designed to be managed and maintained by human sons of God and not human sons of men. This imperfect world is for the sons of men but the coming perfect world shall be for the sons of God only. Natural disasters will cease permanently when the sons of God are revealed on earth.

> "Everything that has been made in the world is waiting for the day when God will make His sons known. [20] Everything that has been made in the world is weak. It is not that the world wanted it to be that way. God allowed it to be that way. Yet there is hope. [21] Everything that has been made in the world will be set free from the power that can destroy. These will become free just as the children of God become free. [22] We know that everything on the earth cries out with pain the same as a woman giving birth to a child. [23] We also cry inside ourselves, even we who have received the Holy Spirit. The Holy Spirit is the first of God's gifts to us. We are waiting to become His complete sons when our bodies are made free."
> Romans 8:19-23 NLV.

Whoever that is eager for natural disasters to cease permanently on earth have got to pray that God should give mankind His godly nature and bring His kingdom over the earth. It is called a natural disaster because it is caused by a nature and it will cease when those two respective natures does not exist any longer.

The only solution to natural disasters is to rid the world and the earthly creations of Satan's evil nature. This is the Good News God gave us through Jesus Christ who He sent into the world. God said He's going to do new thing where He will create new heavens and a new earth with the new kind of human beings who will have the Godly nature and not the evil nature. God will bring His kingdom upon the earth to reign over the earth in true righteousness and there will be everlasting peace and people shall live forever in peace without fear of any natural disaster.

It doesn't sound good both politically and religiously to say this, but the truth is bitter anyways. It is really a painful thing even to God Himself to allow these things to be happening. God is unhappy with all the evil human beings, earth and other earthly natures have to endure to provide evidence for the judgment and condemnation of Satan and the eventual destruction of Satan's evil world. He would have preferred that Satan did not invent evil. Exposing and terminating Satan's evil is for the best of human beings and all earthly natures, therefore the sufferings cannot be compared to the glory that awaits all creations after evil is terminated.

Some people may not like to hear this but it is the truth. The high rate and the wide spread of evil such as these natural disasters gives hope and assurance that God will soon end Satan's evil world. They shows and confirms that Satan's evil nature is unsustainable in God's earth as it does not satisfy God's purpose which the earth and human beings were originally designed for.

Chapter 10

CONCLUSION

"Let us hear the conclusion of the whole matter:
Fear God and keep His commandments, for this is man's all. For God will bring every work into judgment, including every secret thing, whether good or evil."
Ecclesiastes 12:13-14.

God is not happy that we have to experience all these natural disasters. The sufferings, pains, damages and losses from natural disasters are temporary. Though their occurrence is very helpful to our collective desire to see the kingdom of God come upon the earth, the devastation they produce which we have to endure has remained a great burden to our faith in God.

It is helpful to our actual destiny but it is not something we can celebrate. Everything that is getting destroyed by these events were never made to last forever from the beginning. The present universe and all that is in them were created to be dispensable. Everything in this phase of life was made to be temporary in form because God knew that Satan's world is going to be a great disaster.

The anchor and stability of our faith is when we get the concrete understanding that God will recreate everything which these disasters have destroyed including human beings. After Satan's evil nature and evil world are destroyed, God will create everything new in a form that will last forever and that shall never suffer any destruction again. This is the true hope revealed in the Gospel of truth.

The occurrence of these events confirms the reality of our cherished hope. Our hope of eternal glory and dignity is what is actually worth celebrating. Though the reality of this cherished hope is worth celebrating, but the scripture says we should rather consider it a time to be sober, act wisely to get understanding of what God is doing, and what His perfect will is.

Each natural disaster is a confirmation that Satan's evil world is coming to an end. It is a good news which is supposed to make every human being happy. We are rather compelled and constrained by the attendant destructions and loss of life to use it as a time to think and meditate on our faith and on what we are doing to get as many people as possible ready for the end.

The more they happen, the closer the end of this evil world. The closer the end is, the greater the urgency to get people saved because many have become very complacent in this world. We're supposed to be celebrating and rejoicing because the end of this evil world is fast approaching. Nevertheless, the fact that many are not aware of this truth and may get swept away to eternal damnation with the evil one compels us to suspend celebration and rather focus on getting many to come to the knowledge of the truth so as to escape damnation. Presently, celebration will be joyless if there is risk that even one person will be lost.

> "Be very careful, then, how you live — not as unwise but as wise, making the most of every opportunity, because the days are evil. Therefore do not be foolish, but understand what the Lord's will is. Do not get drunk on wine, which leads to debauchery. Instead, be filled with the Spirit, speaking to one another with psalms, hymns, and songs from the Spirit. Sing and make music from your heart to the Lord, always giving thanks to God the Father for everything, in the name of our Lord Jesus Christ."
> Ephesians 5:15-20.

Satan the devil is an accuser, someone who imputes guilt or blame. He's always ready to accuse or blame God and mankind for everything that is his fault. He's also an expert in falsely claiming his failures as a victory. He claims and projects his failure as a victory so that mankind and God should be considered as failures rather than him.

Satan wants us to believe that evil in the world is God's fault and not his fault. He claims to have control over natural processes of earth and the authority to disrupt them at his will to unleash disasters and sufferings against God's earthly creations. His goal has always been to get people to think and believe that God is unable to stop him or his actions.

One thing that is true is that Satan is responsible for the evil in the world. He has no control whatsoever over natural disasters as these events happens as a result of earth's natures reacting against Satan's evil. The existence, rise and spread of evil together with the frequent occurrence of natural disasters in the world works against Satan's evil world and evil rule. Though these events caused the downfall of Satan and guaranteed the coming to an end of his evil world, yet Satan will like to claim otherwise.

It is a common knowledge that every government will do whatever that is within or even outside their control to retain power and remain in authority. There is no doubt therefore that Satan will definitely like to take advantage of these events to retain his reign over the earth if he has such control as he claims. Unfortunately, he doesn't have control over them which is the reason these disasters have continued to happen providing enough evidence that is hastening the end of Satan's world.

Anyone who accuses God of being complicit in the existence of evil in the world is demonstrating believe and faith in Satan's lies. Currently, human beings have 70 years to sojourn in this world. We have been told to pray to God for peace of this world. The peace which the Lord promised us is not the absence of evil or calamities. This is an internal peace which is the power to be calm in the presence of evil because you know and understand what the Lord is doing. This peace that surpasses all understanding comes when people receive the knowledge and understanding of what God is doing in and through this world.

> **"This is what the Lord says: "Let not the wise boast of their wisdom or the strong boast of their strength or the rich boast of their riches, but let the one who boasts boast about this: that they have the understanding to know me, that I am the Lord, who exercises kindness, justice and righteousness on earth, for in these I delight," declares the Lord."**
> Jeremiah 9:23-24.

Understanding God, His plans, His ways and His purpose is the actual source of peace and joy for human beings in this world. Everything that has happened, everything that is happening and everything that shall happen are because the LORD God is doing something to expose evil and the evil one, terminate the existence of evil, judge and condemn the evil one who invented evil nature to truncate God's righteous plan and purpose for mankind and the world.

Every human being and all other creations irrespective of race, gender or belief completely agrees that what is going on is very bad in effect but the truth is that they are good with respect to our hope of eternal glory. Our hope for eternal life of glory will be a mirage if Satan's evil world did not become a total disaster and failure.

Despite being good for our future hope of glorious life, the pains and sufferings associated with these events does not allow us to celebrate them. The failure of Satan's world is not the failure of mankind and is not the failure of God. The failure of Satan's evil world is the victory of God's plan and purpose and also the ultimate victory of human hope of perfection, peace and prosperity.

> "For because of our faith, he has brought us into this place of highest privilege where we now stand, and we confidently and joyfully look forward to actually becoming all that God has had in mind for us to be.
>
> ³ We can rejoice, too, when we run into problems and trials, for we know that they are good for us—they help us learn to be patient. ⁴ And patience develops strength of character in us and

> helps us trust God more each time we use it until finally our hope and faith are strong and steady. [5] Then, when that happens, we are able to hold our heads high no matter what happens and know that all is well, for we know how dearly God loves us, and we feel this warm love everywhere within us because God has given us the Holy Spirit to fill our hearts with his love."
> Romans 5"2-5 TLB.

The scripture says we should rejoice in all things including in the face of suffering, pain and losses because of what they mean for our hope of eternal glory. No matter the amount of efforts and measures that will be taken to address the issue of disasters and sufferings in this world, there will be no end whatsoever to sufferings and disasters unless our human nature is changed to godly nature and the kingdom of God become the world that exist upon the earth.

Finally, as you receive this true knowledge; - *"Rejoice in hope, be patient in tribulation, be constant in prayer."* Romans 12:12 ESV. Jesus has already overcome this world of evil with all its natural disasters. There is a perfect world that is coming in which perfect human beings shall live forever in absolute peace. These perfect human beings are those who shall be made perfect through a new spiritual birth after persevering in faith and truth in this evil world. They are people like you who upon reading this book will believe in God's truth revealed by God's Captain of salvation for mankind who is Jesus Christ.

God brought us into this present evil world for us to serve His purpose. This purpose is to expose in ourselves the evil found in Satan so that enough evidence of evil will be gathered which shall be used to judge and condemn Satan the evil one. God's plan is that after this is done, He will give us a new immortal nature with which we shall enjoy eternal perfect life in His coming glorious world. This coming world is the real perfect and eternal world God planned for mankind before evil was found in Satan's heart.

Every human being shall live twice. Our first phase of life is the temporary one we are currently living in this mortal human form. The second phase will be permanent which we shall live in immortal human form. Jesus came into this world by being born like every other human being. He suffered evil as well because he will be part of the coming world. None of the angels did this. All the heavenly angels who the Father sent into the world came with full grown human bodies unlike Jesus who was conceived in the womb and delivered in birth like every other human being.

"Because God's children are human beings—made of flesh and blood—the Son also became flesh and blood. For only as a human being could he die, and only by dying could he break the power of the devil, who had the power of death. ¹⁵ Only in this way could he set free all who have lived their lives as slaves to the fear of dying.

¹⁶ We also know that the Son did not come to help angels; he came to help the descendants of Abraham. ¹⁷ Therefore, it was necessary for him to be made in every respect like us, his brothers and sisters, so that he could be our merciful and faithful High Priest before God. Then he could offer a sacrifice that would take away the sins of the people. ¹⁸ Since he himself has gone through suffering and testing, he is able to help us when we are being tested."

Hebrews 2:14-18 NLT.

Whoever that is not conceived in this evil world or do not go through this evil world patiently and faithfully shall not be part of the coming perfect world. This current evil world is not the only phase of human existence. In other words, human beings were not designed to just exist only in this phase. This current world is the first phase of human existence. It is the path that brings human beings to the real perfect life and world.

We go through this present temporary life having a nature that is mortal in order to get rid of the corrupted evil nature before receiving the godly nature and come into the real permanent phase of life where evil will completely be absent because the evil one will be held permanently in hellfire.

The status of being called the children of God is the highest status we can attain in this current life. Every human being in this life will need help and assistance from heaven to go through this world. God's Holy Spirit and heavenly servants (Angels) are given to be our helpers, assistance and ministers in this life, but in the coming perfect world, we shall be human sons of God with godly nature (having in us the Spirit of Christ which is God's Spirit of sonship).

In the coming permanent phase of our existence, we shall be given responsibility as human sons of God. As sons, we do not need help or assistance to discharge our responsibility because we shall have the nature of God. The nature of God known as the godly nature will give us the righteousness of God to properly manage and maintain the earth in a way and manner established by God who made the earth for His own pleasure.

"The Spirit Himself bears witness with our spirit that we are children of God, and if children, then heirs—heirs of God and joint heirs with Christ, if indeed we suffer with Him, that we may also be glorified together. For I consider that the sufferings of this present time are not worthy to be compared with the glory which shall be revealed in us. For

> the earnest expectation of the creation eagerly waits for the revealing of the sons of God." Romans 8:16-19.

There is a clear difference between being children of God and being sons of God. Besides Jesus Christ, no human being in this phase of life can attain the status of a son of God which is the reason we need Holy Spirit's help and ministration with Angelic assistance. Children of God are likened to sheep that needs to be cared and provided for while Sons of God like Jesus and Angels do not need help or assistance to discharge their responsibility.

> "Beloved, now we are children of God; and it has not yet been revealed what we shall be, but we know that when He is revealed, we shall be like Him, for we shall see Him as He is." 1 John 3:2.

We shall be like the Christ the Son because then we shall have in us the Spirit of Christ which is the Spirit of God for His sonship.

> "For whom He foreknew, He also predestined to be conformed to the image of His Son, that He might be the firstborn among many brethren." Romans 8:29.

Understanding God, His plans, His ways and His purpose is the actual source of peace and joy for human beings in this world.

Presently, celebration will be joyless if there is risk that even one person will be lost.

About the Author

Celestine Ulasi is a minister of the Gospel chosen and called to provide divine explanation of spiritual truths about God's plans, ways and purpose for all creations in general and mankind in particular.

His works are meant to make people to know and understand all what has been going on in the world so that everyone everywhere despite religion or tradition should enjoy all surpassing peace, live hopefully, faithfully and be very confident about the present time and the eternal future.

The goal is to help people cross the barrier of religion and tradition to know the faithfulness of God's plan and purpose, discover the reality of God's ways and develop a sustainable faith and trust in God through Jesus who is the Christ of God.

All Correspondence to:

Narrow Gate To Life Mission
245 Fairview Mall Dr. #409
Toronto, ON M2J 4T1
Canada.
www.narrowgatetolifemission.org
info@narrowgatetolifemission.org
Celestine_ulasi@narrowgatetolifemission.org

Coming out soon is a book that carefully explains the origin and nature of evil in the world. It provides divinely inspired answer on why there is evil in the world with when and how evil will end.

You can contact us for information on when it will come out and how to obtain a copy or copies.